PURCELL

My heart is inditing

CORONATION ANTHEM (1685)

for ssaatbbb verse, SSAATBBB chorus, strings and continuo

EDITED BY PETER DENNISON

Order No: NOV 070462

NOVELLO PUBLISHING LIMITED

EDITORIAL NOTES

SOURCES

A *GB-Lbl* Royal MS 20.h.8, f. 53v. A fair copy in Purcell's hand throughout. Although it is usually reliable, there are some obvious blemishes and omissions.

B *GB-Lcm* MS 2011, f. 50. An early 18th-century score demonstrably copied from **A**. It is nevertheless useful for the solutions it offers to the problems posed by **A**.

EDITORIAL METHOD

A has provided the copy text for this edition, and all deviations from that source have been detailed in the Commentary. All material in small type, italics or square brackets, and crossed slurs are editorial. Obsolete time-signatures have been modernised and the originals recorded within the edition. Barring has been regularised. The naming of all instrumental and voice parts is editorial; upper case (SATB) refers to chorus parts, and lower case (satb) refers to verse parts. In both sources, the original vocal clefs were G2 for S1, C1 for S2, C2 for A1, C3 for A2, C4 for T, F3 for B1, F4 for B2 and F4 for B3 (G2 means a G clef on the second line from the bottom of the staff). The distribution of clefs among the eight vocal parts is identical to that of Blows's anthem *God spake sometime in visions* (Musica Britannica vii, p. 3) which was also composed for the coronation of James II in 1685. In both anthems the part with the F3 clef has the tessitura of an upper bass part rather than of a lower tenor. All double barlines are original unless recorded otherwise.

14.vn2.3 means bar 14, the third note of the second violin part. Where no source is cited after an entry, that entry refers to **A**.

TEXT: B.C.P. Psalm 45, *vv.* 1, 10 14-16, 11, 17. Psalm 147, *v.* 12. Isaiah 49, *v.* 23.

PROVENANCE: Composed for the coronation of James II on 23 April 1685. 'one of the Anthems Sung at the Coronation of King James the 2d.' **A**.

No title in **A**; 'My heart is inditing of a good matter' **B**.

COMMENTARY

5.vn1: slur over last two quavers only **B**/ 21. vn2: slur over last three notes **B**/ 26: Double bar and *1st* original/ 27: *2d* original, double bar editorial/ 68: Double bar and *1st* original; vn1: sb., thus mechanics of repeat editorial/ 69: *2d* original/ 81.S1.2: originally d″ but altered, almost certainly by Purcell; d″ **B**/ 82.S1.2: originally c″ but altered as above; c″ **B**/ 153.a2.4: no flat, but flat present in bass figuring/ 160: *(quick)* above all parts/ 179-192: a2 stave present but with neither notes nor, with the exception of bar 182, rests **AB**; 179-181 is the end of f. 58 in **A**, and 182-192 is the whole of f. 58v in **A**/ 182-192 (i.e. the whole of f. 58v in **A**): b2 stave present but with neither notes nor rests. It is unlikely that this part is missing as the bass parts of the texture are complete as they stand, and in places b1 and b3 actually double one another./ 193.A2.3: flat to e′ but smudged and perhaps partially erased **A**; this error copied into **B**/ 218.B1.1-4: Purcell seems to have lapsed briefly into the bass clef. He clearly corrected the first two notes, but the second two remain unclear. This reading is probably what Purcell intended. In **B** the second two notes remain a and b natural proving that the scribe copied uncritically./ 228.A1.3-229.3: *into the King's* **A**/ 240: *Symph again*/ 309: This bar is editorial/ 313-321.s1: For one line on f. 60v Purcell wrote this part in the soprano clef C1/ 321-331: b3 and BC compressed on to one stave/ 386-399.va: For one line on f. 63 Purcell wrote this part in the soprano clef C1/ 406-412.A2: Incorrect underlay erased by Purcell but no alternative substituted/ 407.S1: Unclear — smudge on first two beats compounded by tight binding. On the first beat the smudge appears to have been originally f″ and then corrected to a crotchet rest. The second beat appears to have been originally an e″, not the d″ of vn2 **A**/ 414.T.3-4: *mothers* **A**/ 418-423.S2: Text incorrect and erased by Purcell, but no alternative substituted/ 436: Double bar editorial/ 472: Double bar editorial/ 474.S2.3-end: *as the Treble* and part not written out **AB**.

PETER DENNISON
Faculty of Music,
University of Melbourne,
1984

MY HEART IS INDITING

(1685)

Edited by
Peter Dennison

HENRY PURCELL
(1659-95)

9

10

119. V1 & V2; 120. Va: It is suggested that here, and in similar instances, pairs of slurred quavers in the strings be played ♪. to accord with the voice parts.

20

22

Symphony

241

241 Symphony

247

247

253

253

310
Verse
s1
Hark-en O daughter con - si-der, con - si-der, in - cline thine
s2
Hearken O daughter con - si-der, con - si-der, in - cline thine
a1
Hearken O daughter con - si-der, con - si-der,
a2
Hearken O daughter con - si-der, con - si-der,
t
Hearken O daughter con - si-der, con - si-der,
b1
Hearken O daughter con - si-der, con - si-der, in - cline thine
b2
Hearken O daughter con - si-der, con - si-der,
b3
Hearken O daughter con - si-der, con - si-der,
310
Verse
2

thou may'st make prin-ces in all——— lands.

thou may'st make prin-ces in all—— lands.

thou may'st make prin-ces in all——— lands.

thou may'st make prin-ces in all —— lands.

thou may'st make prin-ces in all lands.

thou may'st make prin-ces in all lands.

Ritornello

Ritornello

Printed and bound in Great Britain by
Caligraving Limited Thetford Norfolk

2 3 4 5 6 7 8 9